Sports Stars, Stats, and Stories

BASEBALL STARS, STA

AND STORIES

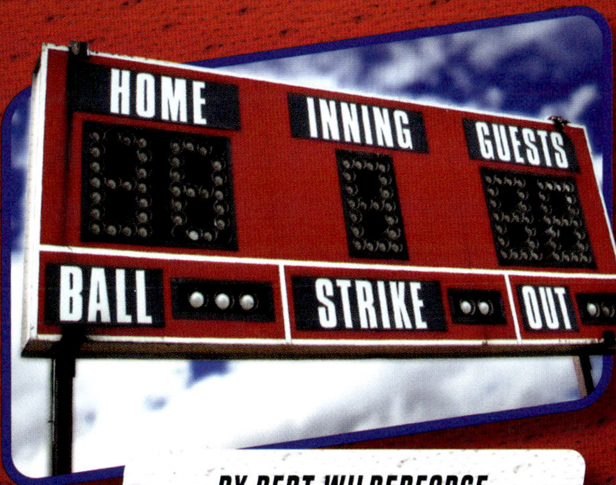

BY BERT WILBERFORCE

Enslow PUBLISHING

INVESTIGATE!

Please visit our website, www.enslow.com. For a free color catalog of all our high-quality books, call toll free 1-800-398-2504 or fax 1-877-980-4454.

Library of Congress Cataloging-in-Publication Data
Names: Wilberforce, Bert, author.
Title: Baseball stars, stats, and stories / Bert Wilberforce.
Description: Buffalo, NY : Enslow Publishing, 2025. | Series: Sports stars, stats, and stories | Includes index.
Identifiers: LCCN 2024030092 (print) | LCCN 2024030093 (ebook) | ISBN 9781978542495 (library binding) | ISBN 9781978542488 (paperback) | ISBN 9781978542501 (ebook)
Subjects: LCSH: Baseball–United States–History–Juvenile literature. | Baseball–United States–Statistics–Juvenile literature.
Classification: LCC GV863.A1 W48 2025 (print) | LCC GV863.A1 (ebook) | DDC 796.357/640973–dc23/eng/20240808
LC record available at https://lccn.loc.gov/2024030092
LC ebook record available at https://lccn.loc.gov/2024030093

Published in 2025 by
Enslow Publishing
2544 Clinton Street
Buffalo, NY 14224

First Edition

Designer: Andrea Davison-Bartolotta
Editor: Therese Shea

Photo credits: Cover, p. 1 (baseball) Dan Thornberg/Shutterstock.com; cover, p. 1 (glove) Dmitry Rukhlenko/Shutterstock.com; cover, pp. 1 (Ohtani), 27 (top) All-Pro Reels/Flickr.com; cover, p. 1 (scoreboard) Lane V. Erickson/Shutterstock.com; cover, p. 1, fact box backgrounds Eugene Onischenko/Shutterstock.com; series art (banners) WinWin artlab/Shutterstock.com; series art (jersey texture) Kwangmoozaa/Shutterstock.com; p. 5 (inset) DatDroneGuy/Shutterstock.com; p. 5 (top) Elliott Cowand Jr/Shutterstock.com; p. 6 Boston Public Library/Flickr.com; p. 7 (bottom) Shawn Collins/Flickr.com; p. 7 (top) Daniel M. Silva/Shutterstock.com; pp. 9, 26, 27 (Judge) apardavila/Flickr.com; pp. 10–11 File:Longest game in professional baseball history - line score.png/Wikimedia Commons; p. 11 The Library of Congress/Flickr.com; p. 12 Steve Starer/Flickr.com; p. 13 (main) File:Lou Gehrig as a new Yankee 11 Jun 1923.jpg/Wikimedia Commons; p. 13 (inset) Joe Haupt/Flickr.com; p. 14 Eric Broder Van Dyke/Shutterstock.com; p. 15 (bottom) Daniel M. Silva/Shutterstock.com; p. 15 (award) Ken Lund/Flickr.com; p. 15 (top) McClatchy-Tribune Information Services/Alamy Live News/Alamy.com; p. 16 Ken Wolter/Shutterstock.com; p. 17 (bottom) File:Satchel Paige 1949 Bowman.jpg/Wikimedia Commons; pp. 17 (top), 18, 19, 20, 29 courtesy of Library of Congress; p. 19 (top graphic) mugiolaris/Shutterstock.com; p. 21 (bottom) John Kim/Flickr.com; p. 21 (top) ArtBrom/Flickr.com; p. 23 (glove only) Cathy T/Flickr.com; p. 23 (field) gigello/Shutterstock.com; p. 25 AP Photo/G. Paul Burnett; p. 26 apardavila/Filckr.com; p. 27 (Acuna) Ian D'Andrea/Flickr.com; p. 28 (all) Tdorante10/ File:FerryHawks vs LI Ducks 2022-09-18 td 329.jpg/WikimediaCommons; p. 29 (logo) File:Logo of the All-American Girls Professional Baseball League.svg/Wikimedia Commons; p. 29 (top) File:Effa Manley Plaque.jpg/Wikimedia Commons.

Printed in the United States of America

INDEX

FOR MORE INFORMATION

BOOKS

Berglund, Bruce. *Baseball GOATs: The Greatest Athletes of All Time.* North Mankato, MN: Capstone Press, 2022.

Berglund, Bruce. *Baseball Records Smashed!* North Mankato, MN: Capstone Press, 2024.

Doeden, Matt. *G.O.A.T. Baseball Teams*. Minneapolis, MN: Lerner Publications, 2021.

WEBSITES

Baseball Reference
www.baseball-reference.com
Check out this great resource for baseball stats and rankings.

National Baseball Hall of Fame
baseballhall.org/hall-of-fame/hall-of-fame-explore
Is your favorite player in the Hall of Fame? Check out the players who are.

The Official Site of Major League Baseball
www.mlb.com
This site has all the news on MLB teams and players.

Publisher's note to educators and parents: Our editors have carefully reviewed these websites to ensure that they are suitable for students. Many websites change frequently, however, and we cannot guarantee that a site's future contents will continue to meet our high standards of quality and educational value. Be advised that students should be closely supervised whenever they access the internet.

CONTENTS

Words in the glossary appear in **bold** type the first time they are used in the text.

THE OLD BALLGAME

Every baseball game is a page in the long story of the sport. Some of the story's heroes were so good they're known even to people who don't follow baseball. Players such as Hank Aaron (755 home runs), Babe Ruth (.690 **slugging percentage**), and Willie Mays (7,112 **putouts** as an outfielder) remain famous years after they stopped playing.

Millions fill the stands each year to watch Major League Baseball (MLB) teams play. As each player comes to bat, fans wonder what will happen next. And anything can happen in baseball!

It takes an entire talented team to win a baseball **championship**, but one player can make a huge difference in a game.

Get the Stats!

As of 2024, the MLB had 30 teams. One, the Toronto Blue Jays, is in Canada.

TORONTO BLUE JAYS STADIUM

WORLD SERIES STUNNERS

The World Series is the championship of Major League Baseball. It's played each year between the champion of the American League (AL) and the champion of the National League (NL). The first one took place in 1903, with the Boston Americans winning over the Pittsburgh Pirates five games to three.

As of 2024, the New York Yankees hold the record for most World Series wins with 27. The St. Louis Cardinals come in second with 11 wins and the Boston Red Sox are third with 9 wins.

BOSTON AMERICANS, 1903 WORLD SERIES

The Yankees also hold the record for playing in the most World Series with 40 appearances.

The modern World Series is a best-out-of-seven series. When teams are tied at three games each, that seventh game is a nail-biter!

The seventh game of the 2016 World Series, between the Cleveland Indians (now, Guardians) and the Chicago Cubs, is one many remember. The Cubs were leading at first, but then the Indians tied it up in the eighth inning. Suddenly, a rainstorm stopped the game for nearly 20 minutes. When play started again, the Cubs scored, winning the World Series for the first time in 108 years.

Get the Stats!

*Just two **no-hitters** have been pitched in World Series history. Yankee Don Larsen threw a **perfect game** in 1959 against the Los Angeles Dodgers. Houston Astro pitchers Cristian Javier, Bryan Abreu, Rafael Montero, and Ryan Pressly combined for a no-hitter in 2022.*

In 2016, the Cubs were losing the World Series three games to one but came back to win.

THE LONGEST GAME

The longest pro baseball game ever wasn't an MLB game. It was a Triple-A game. (Triple-A, or AAA, is the highest level in Minor League Baseball.)

Future MLB stars Wade Boggs and Cal Ripken Jr. were Triple-A players who took part in the longest pro baseball game ever.

The game between the Pawtucket Red Sox and the Rochester Red Wings began around 8 p.m. on April 18, 1981. After 32 innings and more than eight hours of play, it remained tied at 2-2. Play finally stopped at 4 a.m. with a plan to finish on June 23, 1981. And that day, the Red Sox scored a run, winning the game 3-2.

Get the Stats!

The Brooklyn Robins and Boston Braves played the longest MLB game in 1920. It went 26 innings.

BROOKLYN ROBINS PLAYER

THE LONGEST STREAK

As of 2024, each MLB team plays about 162 games in the regular season. It's not easy for players to stay healthy and play every single game.

Between 1925 and 1939, Lou Gehrig, a first baseman for the New York Yankees, played 2,130 games in a row. People called him the "Iron Horse" because of this record. Baltimore Oriole Cal Ripken Jr. broke Gehrig's record in 1995. Ripken, the "Iron Man," holds the current record—2,632 games in a row.

BASEBALL SIGNED BY LOU GEHRIG

Get the Stats!

The MLB season is the longest of any American pro sport.

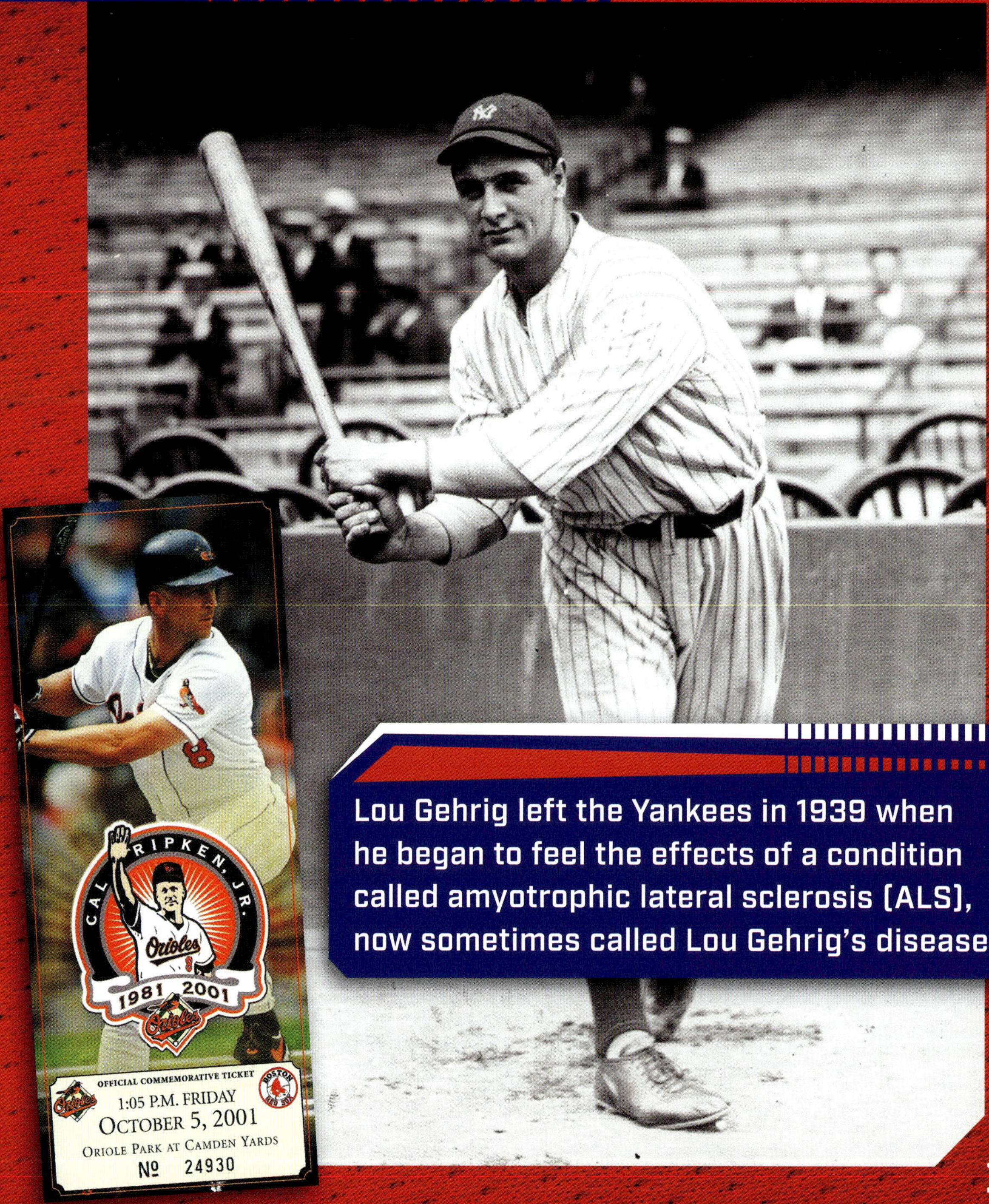

Lou Gehrig left the Yankees in 1939 when he began to feel the effects of a condition called amyotrophic lateral sclerosis (ALS), now sometimes called Lou Gehrig's disease.

PITCHER PERFECT

A pitcher can make or break a game. The Cy Young Award, given to the best pitchers in the NL and AL, is named for Cy Young, the winningest pro pitcher. Between 1890 and 1911, he won 511 games. This record is unlikely to be broken.

Greg Maddux won the Cy Young Award four straight years, from 1992 to 1995, as an Atlanta Brave. During those years, his record was 75-29 with a 1.98 **earned run average** (ERA). He and Young are the only pitchers to have at least 15 wins in 18 seasons.

Get the Stats!

Roger Clemens won seven Cy Young Awards, the most of any pitcher.

GREG MADDUX

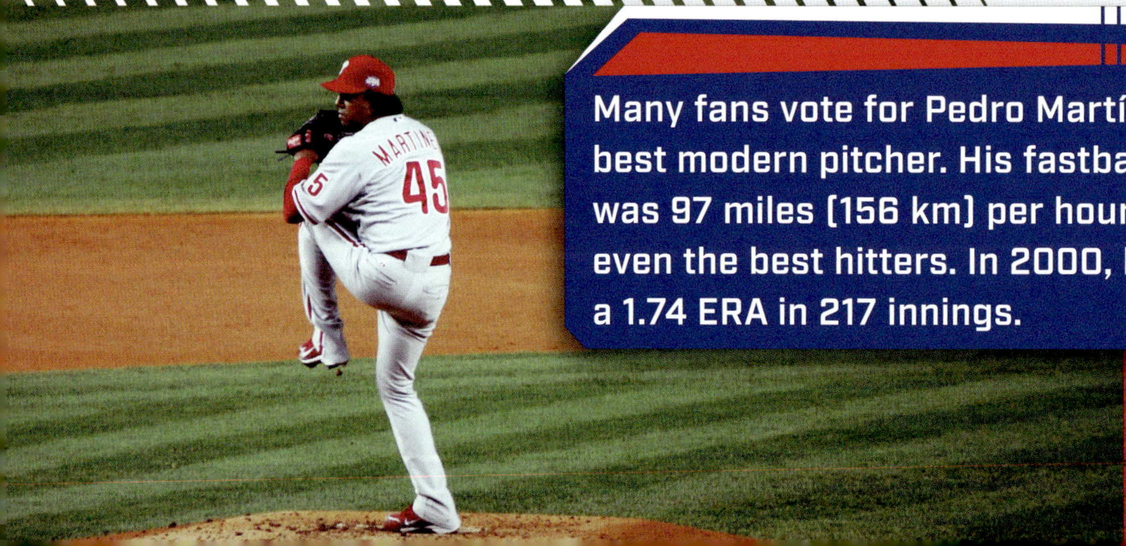

Many fans vote for Pedro Martínez as the best modern pitcher. His fastball, which was 97 miles (156 km) per hour, stopped even the best hitters. In 2000, he posted a 1.74 ERA in 217 innings.

Leroy "Satchel" Paige is often on the greatest pitcher list too. He began in the **Negro leagues** in the 1920s. At that time, the major leagues didn't allow Black players. From 1927 to 1947, Paige won 125 games and lost 82 with a 2.74 ERA and 1,484 **career** strikeouts.

Paige was fun to watch on the field. He kept crowds laughing. Sometimes he told his outfielders to sit down or even go to the bench while he pitched his famous fastballs!

Get the Stats!

In 1971, Satchel Paige became the first Black player chosen for the Baseball Hall of Fame based on his play in the Negro leagues.

PLAYING FOR THE KANSAS CITY MONARCHS

Satchel Paige was one of the first Black players to join the major leagues in 1948. The oldest **rookie** ever, he helped the Cleveland Indians win the World Series that year.

AMERICAN HERO

In 1947, Jackie Robinson became the first Black player to play in the major leagues. The Brooklyn Dodgers second baseman had to deal with problems and even danger because of the color of his skin. Crowds yelled at him. Pitchers threw balls at his body. Some of his own teammates didn't accept him. Robinson bore it all bravely and silently and became Rookie of the Year.

In 1949, Robinson was the NL batting champion with a .342 batting average. He was named the NL Most Valuable Player (MVP).

Over his career, Jackie Robinson had a .311 batting average, 1,518 hits, 137 home runs, 734 runs batted in (RBIs), and 197 stolen bases.

A SHORT HISTORY OF THE MAJOR LEAGUES

1869 THE FIRST PRO BASEBALL TEAM, THE CINCINNATI RED STOCKINGS, BEGINS TO PAY ITS PLAYERS.

1871 NINE TEAMS FORM A PRO BASEBALL LEAGUE.

1876 THE NATIONAL LEAGUE FORMS.

1901 THE AMERICAN LEAGUE FORMS.

1903 THE NL AND AL JOIN TO FORM MAJOR LEAGUE BASEBALL.

1920 THE FIRST SUCCESSFUL NEGRO LEAGUE FORMS FOR BLACK PLAYERS.

1945 JACKIE ROBINSON SIGNS WITH THE MAJOR LEAGUES.

1948 THE NEGRO NATIONAL LEAGUE ENDS.

2024 THE MLB INCLUDES NEGRO LEAGUE RECORDS INTO MLB RECORDS.

Baseball fans and historians have long recognized that the Negro leagues had the same level of talent as the MLB and should be included in the official record books.

Get the Stats!

In 1962, Jackie Robinson had another first—he was the first Black player to enter the Baseball Hall of Fame.

SUPER SLUGGERS

Some batters have the answers to any tricky ball thrown across the plate. The best batters are often ranked by their batting average. Josh Gibson, who played in the Negro leagues, leads all other players with a career .372. Barry Bonds (played 1986-2007) leads in career home runs with 762, and Pete Rose (1963-1986) leads in career hits with 4,256.

Bonds holds the single-season record for home runs too, hitting 73 in 2001. Ichiru Suzuki captured the single-season record for hits in 2004 with 262.

Get the Stats!

For a long time, Ty Cobb topped the career batting average list with .366. In 2024, the MLB accepted Negro league records for the first time, making Gibson the winner.

JOSH GIBSON

BARRY BONDS

Some of baseball's best batters act a certain way to bring themselves luck. For example, before each at-bat, Suzuki pointed his bat toward the pitcher and tugged his shirt (above).

TRIPLE PLAYS

Baseball isn't just about scoring. It's also about defending, or stopping the other team from scoring. Fielders tag runners and make almost impossible catches. Sometimes they work together to make double or even triple plays.

Triple plays, or making three outs in one play, are rare, or uncommon. About 736 have happened since 1876. That's just a few per season. Some kinds are even rarer. An unassisted triple play means one player makes all three outs. This is called the rarest feat in baseball. It's happened only 15 times!

Get the Stats!

In 1990, the Minnesota Twins were the first and only team to make two triple plays in one game.

MOST GOLD GLOVE AWARDS BY POSITION

The MLB gives Gold Glove awards to the best defenders in each position in the American League and in the National League.

FAN-TASTIC TALE

Baseball fans are some of the best sports fans out there. Some fans take their love for their team to the next level. During the first inning of Game 6 of the 1986 World Series, New York Mets fan Michael Sergio **parachuted** into the Mets' Shea Stadium while holding a "Go Mets!" banner. Police quickly took him off the field.

The Mets came from behind to win that game over the Boston Red Sox. The Mets won the championship too.

Get the Stats!

Some Red Sox fans blamed the loss on the "Curse of the Bambino." The Red Sox traded Babe Ruth, nicknamed "the Bambino," to the Yankees in 1919. Some Red Sox fans thought the trade started the 86-season-long championship ***drought*** *that lasted until 2004!*

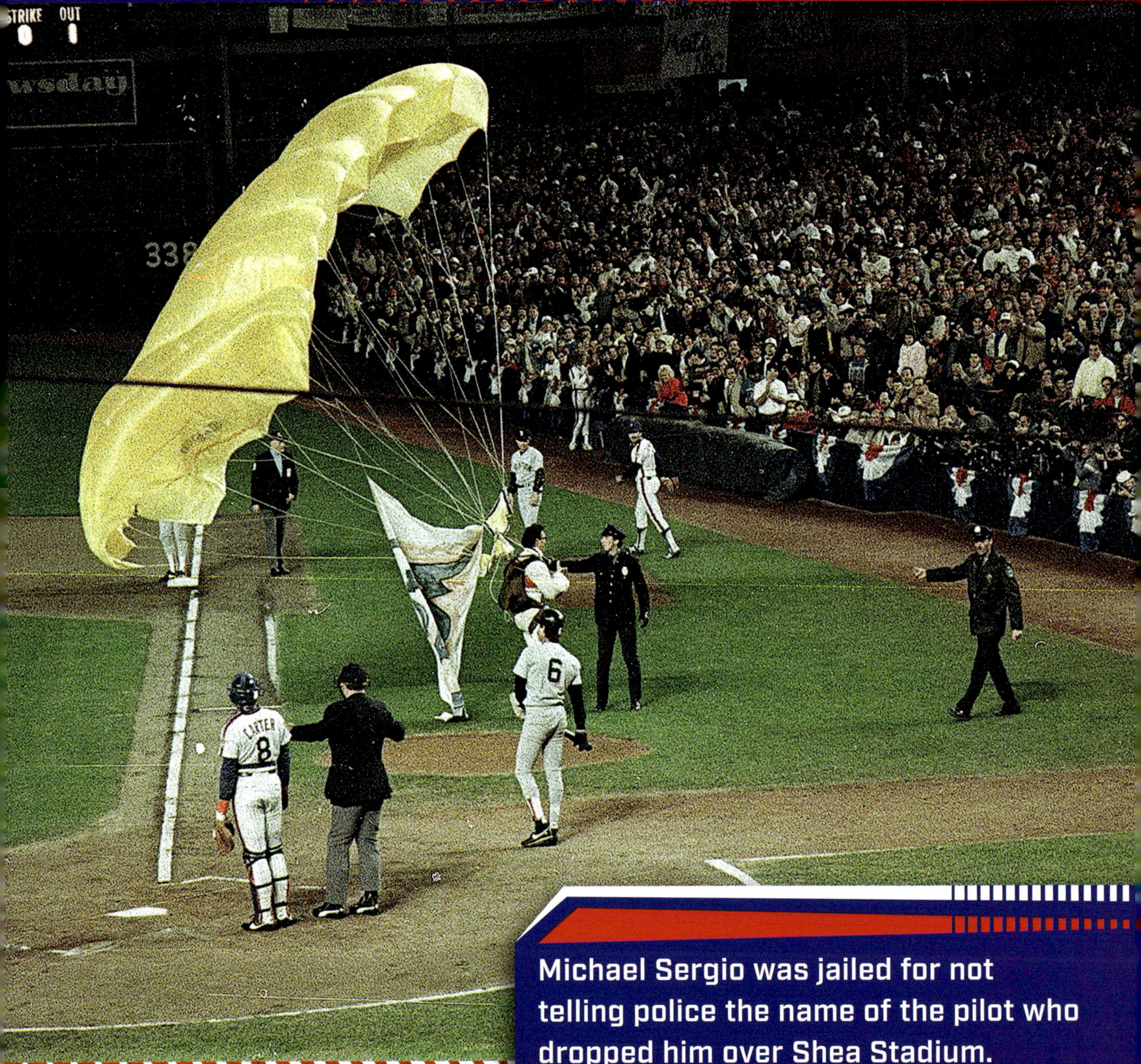

Michael Sergio was jailed for not telling police the name of the pilot who dropped him over Shea Stadium.

STARS OF THE DIAMOND TODAY

Many of the MLB players of today are in the hunt to be record breakers. Yankee Aaron Judge is already one. In 2022, the outfielder set the AL record for most home runs in a season, with 62, and was named the AL MVP.

In 2023, Atlanta Brave Ronald Acuña Jr. made MLB history as the first player to hit at least 40 home runs and steal 70 bases in a season. He was the NL MVP in 2023.

Get the Stats!

In 2020, Mookie Betts became the first player in MLB history to win MVP and the World Series with two different teams before he turned 30 years old.

MOOKIE BETTS

SHOHEI
OHTANI

Shohei Ohtani, a pitcher and **designated hitter,** was the AL MVP for 2021 and 2023. In 2024, he became the first MLB player ever to score 50 home runs and steal 50 bases in one season.

AARON
JUDGE

RONALD
ACUÑA JR.

WOMEN IN BASEBALL

Women have played a part in baseball history—when they were allowed to. In 1931, minor league pitcher Jackie Mitchell struck out Babe Ruth in a special game. The next week, the head of the MLB banned women from playing.

Women's roles in baseball are increasing now. More women are coaching, managing, and owning MLB teams. In 2022, Kelsie Whitmore became the first woman to play in the MLB when she took the field for the minor league Staten Island FerryHawks. The future looks bright for women in baseball!

KELSIE WHITMORE

Effa Manley is the first and only woman in the Baseball Hall of Fame. She was an owner of a Negro league team, the Newark Eagles, and worked for Black players' **civil rights**.

Get the Stats!

Between 1943 and 1954, more than 600 women played in the All-American Girls Professional Baseball League.

GLOSSARY

career: The whole amount of time someone spends at a job.

championship: Events that decide the overall winner of a sport or contest.

civil rights: The personal freedoms granted to U.S. citizens by law.

designated hitter: A baseball player who is named the batter who will take the pitcher's place at bat.

drought: A long period of something expected not happening.

earned run average: The number of earned runs allowed by a pitcher, divided by the number of innings pitched, then multiplied by nine. The lower the number, the better.

Negro league: Any of the groups of African American baseball teams that played mostly between 1920 and the late 1940s. Negro is a word once used for Black people that is often considered offensive today.

no-hitter: A game in which a pitcher goes the whole game without letting a batter hit safely onto base.

parachute: To drop from an aircraft with a special cloth that slows the fall.

perfect game: A game in which a pitcher pitches every inning in a complete game with no opposing batter ever reaching base under any conditions.

putout: When a fielder makes an out.

rookie: A player during their first year in the league.

slugging percentage: The number of bases a batter gets from hits divided by opportunities at bat.